The KidHaven Health Library

What Happens When Someone Has

ANXIETY?

By Katie Kawa

KidHaven PUBLISHING

Published in 2020 by
KidHaven Publishing, an Imprint of Greenhaven Publishing, LLC
353 3rd Avenue
Suite 255
New York, NY 10010

Designer: Andrea Davison-Bartolotta
Editor: Katie Kawa

Photo credits: Cover cheapbooks/Shutterstock.com; pp. 5, 29 Monkey Business Images/Shutterstock.com; p. 6 New Africa/Shutterstock.com; p. 7 (right) Rawpixel.com/Shutterstock.com; p. 7 (left) Daisy Daisy/Shutterstock.com; p. 10 StasyKID/Shutterstock.com; p. 11 iJeab/Shutterstock.com; p. 12 Focus and Blur/Shutterstock.com; p. 13 Ilya Studio/Shutterstock.com; pp. 14, 17 fizkes/Shutterstock.com; p. 15 Bearnika/Shutterstock.com; p. 16 YanLev/Shutterstock.com; p. 18 CI Photos/Shutterstock.com; p. 19 Blamb/Shutterstock.com; p. 20 nednapa/Shutterstock.com; p. 21 Tero Vesalainen/Shutterstock.com; p. 22 Elle Aon/Shutterstock.com; p. 23 Olimpik/Shutterstock.com; p. 24 Pixel-Shot/Shutterstock.com; p. 25 siam.pukkato/Shutterstock.com; p. 28 (top) JStone/Shutterstock.com; p. 28 (middle) Andrea Raffin/Shutterstock.com; p. 28 (bottom) Tinseltown/Shutterstock.com.

Cataloging-in-Publication Data

Names: Kawa, Katie.
Title: What happens when someone has anxiety? / Katie Kawa.
Description: New York : KidHaven Publishing, 2020. | Series: The KidHaven health library | Includes glossary and index.
Identifiers: ISBN 9781534532618 (pbk.) | ISBN 9781534532458 (library bound) | ISBN 9781534532670 (6 pack) | ISBN 9781534532533 (ebook)
Subjects: LCSH: Anxiety in children–Juvenile literature. | Anxiety–Juvenile literature.
Classification: LCC BF723.A5 K39 2020 | DDC 152.4'6–dc23

Printed in the United States of America

CPSIA compliance information: Batch #BW20KL: For further information contact Greenhaven Publishing LLC, New York, New York at 1-844-317-7404.

Please visit our website, www.greenhavenpublishing.com. For a free color catalog of all our high-quality books, call toll free 1-844-317-7404 or fax 1-844-317-7405.

Contents

WHEN TO WORRY ABOUT WORRYING

Everyone experiences anxiety at different points in their lives. It's **normal** to feel anxious before a big test, on your first day at a new school, or after seeing a scary movie.

Although anxiety is part of life, some people experience it more often than others. In some cases, their anxiety makes it hard for them to take part in everyday activities, such as going to school or spending time with friends. When this happens, a person might have an anxiety disorder. This is a health problem that happens when a person's anxiety is excessive, or too strong, for the situations they're facing.

People with an anxiety disorder often worry that they'll feel worried forever. However, there are many ways to help people with anxiety feel better!

More Common Than We Think

Anxiety disorders are the most common **mental** health disorders in the United States. Around 40 million American adults have an anxiety disorder. In addition, anxiety affects around one out of every eight kids in the United States. Girls and women are **diagnosed** with anxiety disorders more often than boys and men.

Anxiety is more than just being worried. It's a sense of worry that's so strong it can cause other problems in the body, such as shaking hands, an increased heart rate, and trouble sleeping.

A SERIOUS PROBLEM

Anxiety is a serious health problem that affects many parts of a person's life. People who are dealing with it need the same respect and support as people who are dealing with **physical** health problems, such as heart problems or the flu.

Different Kinds of Doctors

In many cases, if a person thinks they have a mental disorder such as an anxiety disorder, they see their regular doctor first. However, they can also see doctors who are trained to deal with mental disorders. A psychologist is a doctor who deals with mental health but can't give someone medicine. A psychiatrist is a doctor who can give someone medicine for a mental health problem.

Mental disorders, or mental illnesses, such as anxiety are often treated the same way as physical illnesses—with trips to the doctor and medicine. However, some people with anxiety don't get the **treatment** they need because they're afraid to ask for help. It's important for them to know that there's nothing to be ashamed of. Seeing a doctor for anxiety is no different than seeing a doctor for a cough that won't go away. No one should be judged for taking care of their health, and this includes their mental health.

It's not always easy to tell if someone has a mental disorder. They don't have a fever or a cough, but that doesn't mean their illness isn't real or serious.

STUDYING THE SYMPTOMS

There are different kinds of anxiety disorders, and they each have their own symptoms, or signs. However, most anxiety disorders have some symptoms in common. For example, most people with an anxiety disorder worry more than necessary for a given situation. They always feel as if something bad is going to happen, so they watch for signs of danger and are often jumpy.

Physical symptoms are also common for people with anxiety disorders. Sweating, shortness of breath, and tense, or tight, muscles are all physical signs that someone might be anxious.

An anxiety disorder can cause some people to feel very tired, while it can cause others to feel restless, or on edge. People with an anxiety disorder can also be irritable, which means they get angry quickly.

Other Health Problems

Doctors have made connections between anxiety and other health problems. Anxiety can make heart problems worse, and it can play a part in migraines, which happen when a person experiences serious headaches, or pain in the head. Anxiety disorders cause stomach problems too. A skin condition called eczema, which causes the skin to become red and itchy, can also be made worse by anxiety.

Common Anxiety Symptoms

mental and emotional symptoms	physical symptoms
excessive worrying	racing heart
being unable to control worrying	shortness of breath
feeling as if something bad is always about to happen	sweating
feeling restless	tense muscles
feeling irritable	headaches
feeling afraid when there is no current danger	stomach problems
constantly watching for signs of danger	feeling tired

If a person has any of these symptoms for a short period of time, they might be feeling anxious but most likely don't have an anxiety disorder. However, if their worrying lasts for a long time and they have other symptoms too, they should talk to a doctor about their anxiety.

FEELING ANXIOUS ALL THE TIME

Some people have anxiety about certain things or situations, while others feel anxious almost all the time. When someone feels excessive anxiety most days for a period of six months or longer, they might have generalized anxiety disorder (GAD).

A person with GAD often worries about many parts of everyday life, such as their family, their health, the weather, and their work. Although most people worry about these things from time to time, someone with GAD worries about them even when there's no reason to. They can't control their worrying, which can

Wide Awake

GAD and other anxiety disorders often cause people to have trouble sleeping. Some people with anxiety have trouble falling asleep because they can't stop worrying. Others wake up in the middle of the night and can't fall back to sleep. These kinds of sleep problems are known as insomnia.

last for hours every day as they plan for the worst to happen. This makes it hard for someone with GAD to deal with normal activities, and it can make them feel very tired.

Both adults and children can have GAD. People with this disorder often have a hard time in situations where they don't know what's going to happen. They also feel very anxious about making decisions. Having a support system of understanding friends and family members is important for them.

WHEN FEAR TAKES OVER

While people with GAD feel worry or fear most of the time, some people only experience excessive anxiety about **specific** things or situations. This is known as a phobia. Someone with a phobia feels a high level of fear when there's no need for it. For example, a person with a phobia may have a fear of spiders even though they know most spiders they see won't harm them.

Needing to Escape

Agoraphobia is the fear of being unable to leave a place or situation. People with this disorder are often afraid they're going to start to panic and won't be able to escape. They often feel excessive anxiety in crowds, as well as in spaces that are very open or places that are hard to exit, such as trains or movie theaters. If agoraphobia goes untreated, it can make it hard for someone to leave their house by themselves.

Everyone is afraid of certain things, but people with phobias let this fear affect their daily lives. They often do whatever they can to avoid the thing they're afraid of, even if it makes them unhappy or causes problems for their loved ones. Someone with a fear of flying in an airplane might never travel because of their phobia.

A person with a phobia generally knows their fears are irrational, or unreasonable. However, they have a mental disorder that makes it hard for them to control their fear without the right treatment. This is why telling them there's nothing to be afraid of generally doesn't help.

SCARY SOCIAL SITUATIONS

Some people have a specific fear of being in social situations. This is known as social anxiety disorder. Someone living with social anxiety disorder has an intense, or strong, fear of dealing with people that lasts for at least six months. They often do whatever they can to avoid social situations, which means they miss out on time with family and friends. They also avoid speaking in class or at work.

Separation Anxiety

Children often have a hard time being separated from their parents, but in some cases, this fear of separation is a sign of a serious anxiety disorder. Separation anxiety disorder occurs when someone is so afraid that something bad will happen to someone they care about that they can't be apart from them without experiencing intense anxiety. This disorder is often seen in children, but adults can also have separation anxiety.

Some people mistake social anxiety disorder for shyness. It's actually much more serious. Social anxiety disorder can make it hard for someone to go to school or work, and it can affect their relationships. When someone with this disorder has to take part in a social situation, their anxiety can make them feel very uncomfortable or even sick.

A person with social anxiety disorder is often afraid that people will make fun of them or that they'll do something **embarrassing**, even if there's no reason to believe this will happen.

DEALING WITH PANIC ATTACKS

People with anxiety disorders sometimes experience panic attacks. During a panic attack, a person may experience very strong physical symptoms of anxiety, including shortness of breath, increased heart rate, chest pain, dizziness, shaking, and sweating. They may feel as if they're losing control of themselves or even that they're going to die. In some cases, they believe they're having a heart attack, so they go to the hospital.

A Helping Hand

It can be scary to watch someone have a panic attack, but there are things you can do to help them. The most important thing you can do is stay calm and not leave them alone. Ask the person how you can help, and get help from a trusted adult if you can. You can also help them slow down their breathing by taking deep breaths with them.

Panic attacks are scary, but they generally don't cause lasting harm to the body. However, it's still important to see a doctor if you're having panic attacks because they can help stop the attacks from happening.

Panic attacks are often over in minutes, but the fear of having another one can last for a long time. Someone with panic disorder has frequent panic attacks that come without warning. They feel so anxious about having another attack that it affects their daily activities because they want to avoid anything that might cause them to panic.

FIGHT-OR-FLIGHT

What causes panic attacks and other symptoms of anxiety disorders? The human body is built to **react** to danger with what's often known as the fight-or-flight **response**. This is controlled by a part of the brain called the amygdala. When the amygdala senses danger, it sends messages to prepare the body to either fight the danger or run away from it. This is what causes the increased heart rate, shaking, and shortness of breath often experienced with anxiety.

Sending Messages

Nerve cells in the brain—also called neurons—send messages to one another using chemicals called neurotransmitters. These messages control how people learn, talk, and deal with emotions. Doctors believe these chemicals play a part in anxiety disorders. Low levels of certain neurotransmitters cause feelings of anxiety, so some medicines for anxiety work to balance the levels of these chemicals in the brain.

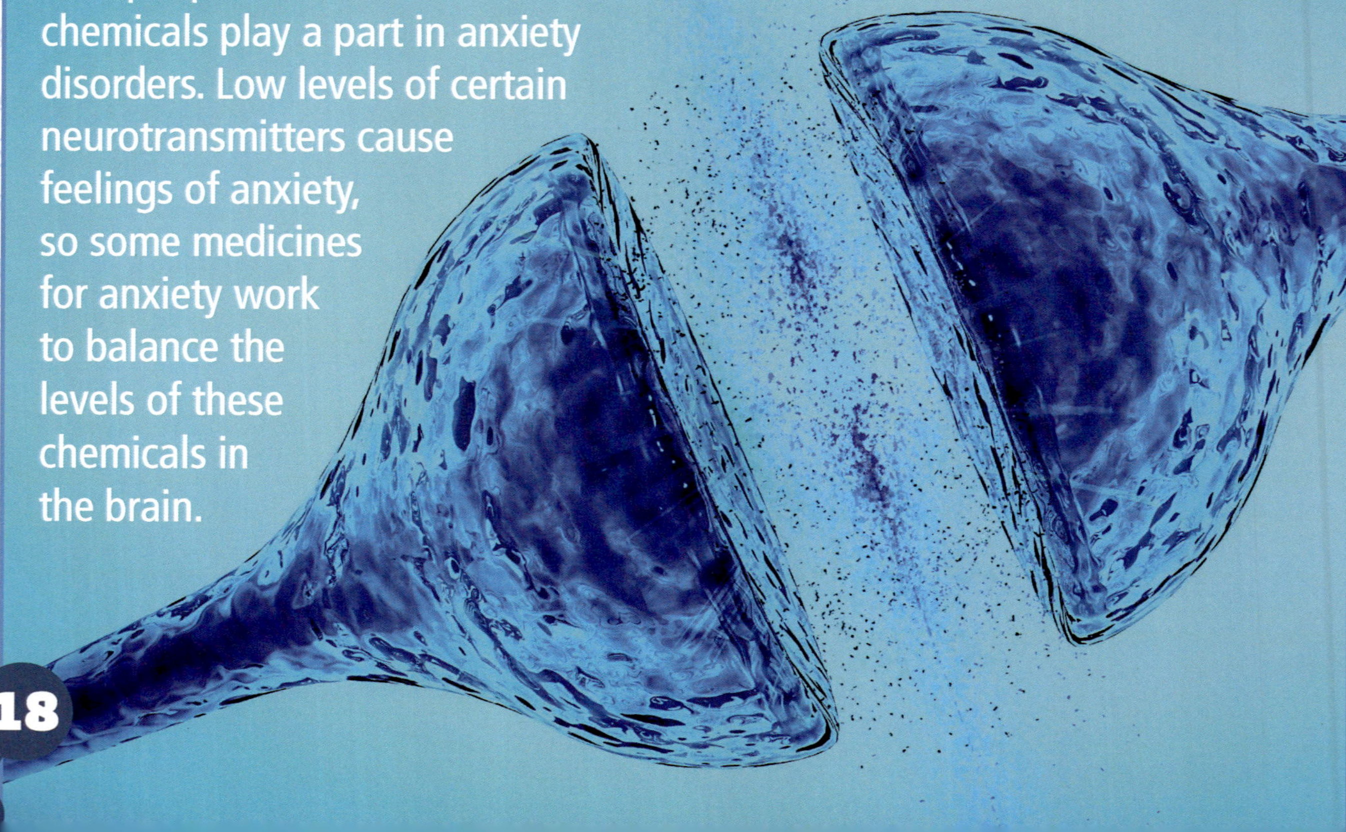

In most cases of anxiety, though, the amygdala is reacting to something that's not actually harmful. However, the fight-or-flight response kicks in before the cerebral cortex—the part of the brain that deals with logic and reason—can figure out that there's no real danger.

The amygdala also helps create memories. When it activates the fight-or-flight response, it sometimes creates a memory of something being scary even though it wasn't a real danger.

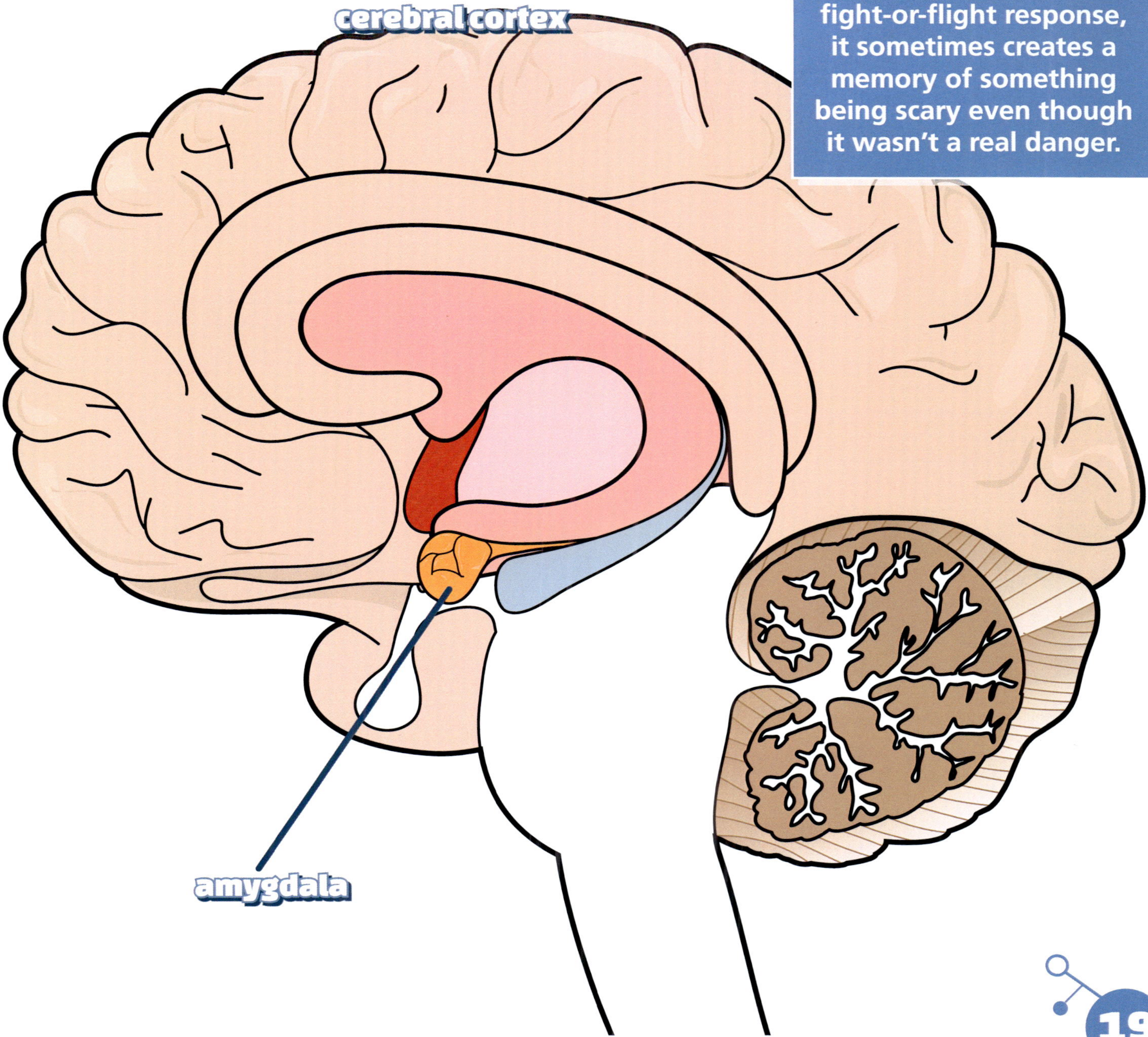

A COMBINATION OF CAUSES

Doctors are still working to figure out why some people **develop** anxiety disorders and some don't. They believe genes might play a part. Genes control different things about a person, such as their eye color and how likely they are to have certain disorders. Genes are passed down from parents to their children. Because anxiety disorders often run in families, doctors believe some genes might make people more likely to develop an anxiety disorder.

Many experts—people who know a lot about anxiety disorders—believe genes and life experiences work together to cause an anxiety disorder to develop. Doctors around the world are working to learn more about the science of anxiety so they can better understand what causes it and how to treat it.

In addition, scary life experiences, such as a car accident or the death of a loved one, can lead to problems with anxiety. Being sick or under a lot of **stress** for a long period of time can also cause some people to develop an anxiety disorder.

Taking Triggers Seriously

Many people with anxiety disorders can name certain things that cause them to have anxious feelings or panic attacks. These things are called triggers. For example, seeing a spider might trigger a panic attack for a person with a phobia, and a public speaking project might trigger someone's social anxiety. It's important to respect someone when they say something triggers their anxiety. Making them face their fears without the help of a doctor can be harmful.

TALKING THROUGH IT

The first step to feeling better is often seeing a doctor. This is true with both physical and mental health problems. Only a doctor can officially diagnose someone with an anxiety disorder and come up with a treatment plan for them.

Many people with anxiety disorders find talk therapy helpful. This is a kind of treatment in which a doctor or another trained mental health worker—often called a therapist—

Facing Your Fears

Another kind of therapy that can help people with anxiety is exposure therapy, in which doctors help people face their fears in a safe way. For example, if someone's phobia deals with public speaking, their doctor will help them become more comfortable speaking in front of people so they no longer avoid this activity. In some cases, doctors use **virtual reality** to expose their patients to situations such as being on an airplane.

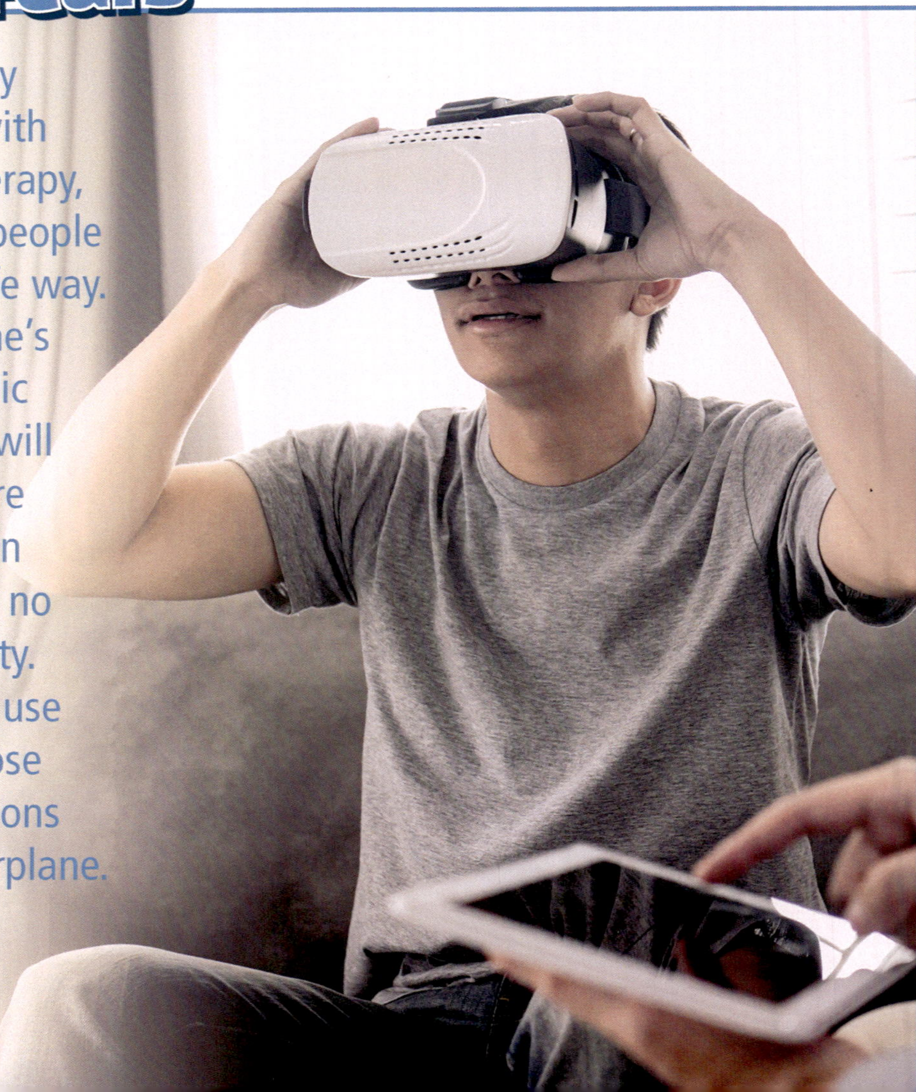

helps a person talk about problems in their lives and work through those problems.

Cognitive behavioral therapy (CBT) is often used to treat people with anxiety disorders. This kind of therapy deals with changing how people react to situations that cause them anxiety. They learn to handle these situations in a healthier way.

Finding the right therapist isn't always easy. Sometimes a person has to visit a few different therapists to find someone who's a good fit for them. This is important because a person with anxiety needs to be able to trust their therapist.

MEDICINE FOR ANXIETY

Anxiety is often treated with a combination of therapy and medicine. Taking medicine for anxiety is a lot like taking medicine for a cold. It won't cure the person dealing with this health problem, but it often helps to lessen their symptoms so they can deal with everyday life more comfortably.

Other Kinds of Treatments

Many people who live with anxiety disorders find other kinds of treatments helpful too. Exercise is believed to help people with many health problems, including anxiety. One kind of exercise, known as yoga, can be very helpful for dealing with anxiety. When people practice yoga, they do different stretches while breathing deeply. This can help relax the brain and body.

Some medicines for anxiety work to quickly calm a person, but they're generally only used for a short period of time or as needed. Other anxiety medicines are also used to treat another mental health disorder known as **depression**. These medicines work to balance brain chemicals that play a part in both depression and anxiety.

People should follow their doctor's orders when taking these medicines. They should also never stop taking them without talking to their doctor first.

Doctors work with their patients to find the right kind of medicine and the right amount, or dosage, to help them feel better.

SHOWING SUPPORT

It's not easy to live with anxiety. Bullies sometimes pick on people for being afraid of things, and many people don't understand that anxiety isn't something a person can easily get over by thinking positively. It takes hard work and treatment to deal with an anxiety disorder. It also takes support from family and friends.

If you know someone who's dealing with anxiety, you can support them by treating them with respect and kindness. Don't make fun of the things people worry about. Even if something doesn't seem scary to you, it can be very scary for someone with an anxiety disorder. People with anxiety are sometimes embarrassed about their disorder, but you can remind them that anxiety isn't a sign of weakness.

What Not to Say

Sometimes, people think they're offering good advice to someone with an anxiety disorder, but they're actually not being very helpful. For example, telling someone with anxiety to calm down is like telling someone with a cold to stop sneezing. An anxiety disorder makes it hard for a person to be calm, even when they know there's no reason to panic. They can't control their anxiety, so telling them to control it doesn't work.

How can you help someone with anxiety?

! Ask them if they need help with tasks such as practicing giving a report.

! Do yoga or another kind of exercise with them.

! Learn more about anxiety disorders.

! If they're having a panic attack, find an adult or stay with them and help them slow down their breathing until it's over.

! Treat them with kindness, and never make fun of their fears.

! Listen respectfully when they talk about their anxiety.

! Use supportive language when they're anxious instead of telling them there's nothing to worry about.

People often think it's helpful to tell someone with anxiety that their fears are all in their head, but that generally doesn't make them feel better. Instead, you can try some of these ideas for supporting someone with anxiety.

TAKING BACK CONTROL

Millions of people around the world deal with anxiety, and it affects kids as well as adults. In fact, symptoms of anxiety disorders often start showing up early in a person's life. If you're having a hard time dealing with anxiety, you're not alone. Tell a trusted adult, and remember that asking for help is a very brave thing to do.

Speaking Out About Anxiety

Many people believe that speaking out about their experience with anxiety can help others feel less alone. These include famous people, such as Emma Stone, Chris Evans, Lili Reinhart, and Ryan Reynolds. However, if someone with anxiety doesn't feel comfortable talking about their disorder, they don't have to talk about it. Sharing stories about your mental health is a personal choice that no one should make for you.

When someone has an anxiety disorder, it can feel as if their worries are controlling their life. However, they don't have to lose hope. They can start feeling better when they get the help they need. Anxiety disorders generally don't go away on their own, but with the right treatment, people with anxiety can control their worries instead of letting their worries control them.

The world can sometimes be a scary place, but it's also a place that's full of fun. When someone gets help for an anxiety disorder, they learn to focus more on the fun and less on the fear.

Glossary

depression: A mental illness with signs that include sadness, hopelessness, and a lack of interest in doing things that were once considered enjoyable.

develop: To cause something to change, happen, or be created over time.

diagnose: To identify a disease by its signs and symptoms.

embarrassing: Causing a feeling of foolishness.

mental: Relating to the mind.

normal: Usual.

physical: Relating to the body.

react: To behave in a certain way when something happens.

response: Something done as a reaction to something that has happened.

specific: Special or particular.

stress: Something that causes strong feelings of worry.

treatment: Care given to a person or animal that is sick.

virtual reality: An artificial, digital world made of images and sounds that is affected by the actions of the person who is experiencing it.

For More Information

WEBSITES

Child Mind Institute: #MyYoungerSelf
childmind.org/myyoungerself/
The videos on this website feature many famous people talking about their own struggles with mental health problems, such as anxiety, and what advice they'd give their younger selves.

KidsHealth: Feelings
kidshealth.org/en/kids/feeling
This part of the KidsHealth website deals with feelings, including feelings of anxiety and stress.

BOOKS

Cook-Cottone, Catherine, and Rebecca K. Vujnovic. *Mindfulness for Anxious Kids: A Workbook to Help Children Cope with Anxiety, Stress, and Worry.* Oakland, CA: Instant Help Books, 2018.

Duhig, Holly. *Understanding Anxiety.* New York, NY: PowerKids Press, 2019.

Spalding, Maddie. *12 Tips for Managing Stress and Anxiety.* Mankato, MN: 12-Story Library, 2017.

Index